TECHNICAL REPORT

Prebankruptcy Credit Counseling

Noreen Clancy, Stephen J. Carroll

Prepared for the National Institute of Justice

RAND Safety and Justice

A RAND INFRASTRUCTURE, SAFETY, AND ENVIRONMENT PROGRAM

This research was sponsored by the National Institute of Justice at the request of the Executive Office for U.S. Trustees and was conducted within the auspices of the Safety and Justice Program within RAND Infrastructure, Safety, and Environment.

Library of Congress Cataloging-in-Publication Data

Clancy, Noreen.
  Prebankruptcy credit counseling / Noreen Clancy, Stephen J. Carroll.
    p. cm.
  Includes bibliographical references.
  ISBN-13: 978-0-8330-4205-7 (pbk. : alk. paper)
  1. Consumer credit—Management. 2. Bankruptcy—Prevention. I. Carroll, Stephen J., 1940– II. Title.

HG3755.C525 2007
332.7'43—dc22

2007029527

The RAND Corporation is a nonprofit research organization providing objective analysis and effective solutions that address the challenges facing the public and private sectors around the world. RAND's publications do not necessarily reflect the opinions of its research clients and sponsors.

RAND® is a registered trademark.

Published 2007 by the RAND Corporation
1776 Main Street, P.O. Box 2138, Santa Monica, CA 90407-2138
1200 South Hayes Street, Arlington, VA 22202-5050
4570 Fifth Avenue, Suite 600, Pittsburgh, PA 15213-2665
RAND URL: http://www.rand.org/
To order RAND documents or to obtain additional information, contact
Distribution Services: Telephone: (310) 451-7002;
Fax: (310) 451-6915; Email: order@rand.org

Preface

The Bankruptcy Abuse Prevention and Consumer Protection Act of 2005 (BAPCPA) requires that any individual who files for bankruptcy must have received credit counseling within the 180-day period prior to filing. The U.S. Trustee Program (USTP)[1] was charged with approving nonprofit agencies to provide this counseling service and with annually reapproving all such providers.

To meet this mandate, USTP must develop criteria for measuring the effectiveness of counseling-agency services to evaluate agencies for approval or reapproval. Accordingly, USTP needs to develop operational measures of the effectiveness of prebankruptcy credit counseling.

USTP asked the RAND Corporation for assistance in examining what constitutes effective prebankruptcy credit counseling and how it can be measured. This technical report provides the results of RAND's assessment of these issues.

This research was sponsored by the National Institute of Justice at the request of EOUST. This research would be of interest to policymakers concerned with bankruptcy issues, bankruptcy practitioners, and the credit and credit-counseling industries.

The RAND Safety and Justice Program

This research was conducted under the auspices of the Safety and Justice Program within RAND Infrastructure, Safety, and Environment (ISE). The mission of ISE is to improve the development, operation, use, and protection of society's essential physical assets and natural resources and to enhance the related social assets of safety and security of individuals in transit and in their workplaces and communities. Safety and Justice Program research addresses occupational safety, transportation safety, food safety, and public safety—including violence, policing, corrections, substance abuse, and public integrity.

Questions or comments about this report should be sent to the authors, Noreen Clancy (Noreen_Clancy@rand.org) and Stephen Carroll (Stephen_Carroll@rand.org). Information about the Safety and Justice Program is available online (http://www.rand.org/ise/safety). Inquiries about research projects should be sent to the following address:

---

[1] USTP is the component of the U.S. Department of Justice with the mission of promoting the integrity and efficiency of the bankruptcy system by enforcing bankruptcy laws. USTP is managed by the Executive Office for U.S. Trustees (EOUST).

Andrew Morral, Director
Safety and Justice Program, ISE
RAND Corporation
1200 South Hayes Street
Arlington, VA 22202-5050
703-413-1100, x5119
Andrew_Morral@rand.org

Contents

Summary

Introduction

The Bankruptcy Abuse Prevention and Consumer Protection Act of 2005 (BAPCPA) provided new requirements for bankruptcy filers and gave the U.S. Trustee Program (USTP) new areas of responsibility. One of the new requirements is that any individual who files for bankruptcy must have received credit counseling during the 180 days prior to filing. When a consumer completes such prebankruptcy credit counseling, he or she receives a certificate that must be submitted at the time of bankruptcy filing.

USTP is now faced with having to decide whether to reapprove or remove agencies that are on the approved list of credit-counseling agencies. To do this, USTP must develop criteria for measuring the effectiveness of counseling-agency services that may be used to evaluate whether agencies qualify for approval or reapproval. Complicating the issue of effectiveness is the increased use of Internet-based credit counseling and whether the mode of delivery, particularly delivery through the Internet, affects the adequacy and effectiveness of the counseling provided.

The basic questions that the Executive Office for U.S. Trustees (EOUST), which manages USTP, is attempting to explore related to prebankruptcy credit counseling are as follows:

- What constitutes effective credit counseling in the prebankruptcy context?
- What are appropriate operational measures of effective prebankruptcy credit counseling?
- Does the mode of delivery of prebankruptcy credit counseling, particularly delivery through the Internet, influence the effectiveness of the counseling?

USTP asked RAND for assistance in examining the issue of what constitutes effective prebankruptcy credit counseling and how it could be measured. We reviewed the relevant literature that could inform the three questions and consulted with a bankruptcy study group of academic, government, and private-sector experts formed as part of a joint National Institute of Justice–USTP (NIJ-USTP) project to study bankruptcy fraud, abuse, and error to get feedback on the literature-review results.

Conclusions

To address these questions and to eventually develop operational measures of effectiveness, we conclude that **USTP's first step should be to explicitly identify the goals of prebankruptcy credit counseling. The other suggestions depend on the goals being defined.**

Even if goals are defined, we conclude that **there are no common standards or accepted sets of metrics for USTP to adopt in whole as it attempts to assess prebankruptcy credit-counseling agencies, but there may be many transferable pieces from some of the research studies reviewed**. Although many of the approaches had similarities, every field approached the assessment of effectiveness somewhat differently based on its specific goals.

We also conclude that **there are no accepted views on the various modes of delivery. The research shows that the effectiveness of the modes seems to vary depending on the type of counseling being delivered and its purpose**. More specifically, we found no empirical research on the effectiveness of Internet delivery of prebankruptcy credit counseling, nor did we discover relevant studies from the fields of credit counseling, financial literacy, or pre-purchase homeownership counseling. Most of the available research studies relating to delivery of information through the Internet are geared toward higher education, and we conclude that this research has little transferable value. Additionally, we did not come across instances in which this delivery method was used to handle specific personal information. Whether an online session alone, which by its nature is somewhat standardized, can effectively take into account an individual's specific financial situation and all its nuances is questionable. The blended programs in which online sessions are paired with telephone calls with actual counselors could be an effective method but should be studied further.

Recommendations

Based on these conclusions, we recommend that USTP use a series of upcoming reviews and reports to help it inform the processes of developing operational measures of effectiveness and of approving or reapproving credit-counseling agencies. These include its own quality service reviews, the results of ongoing work by Staten and Barron (2006) that should lend insight into operational measures of prebankruptcy credit counseling, and the results of the upcoming National Foundation for Credit Counseling (NFCC) Outcomes and Impact Task Force to develop performance metrics to assess the effectiveness of its counseling and education services.

There are other suggestions that USTP may want to consider as it contemplates reapproving providers and develops a process for constructing operational measures of effectiveness. These suggestions, which stem from discussions at the study-group meeting and are expanded in this report, include the following:

- In evaluating agencies for reapproval, consider whether the agency is providing the services stated in its application to become an approved credit-counseling agency. Also consider any pre- and post-testing that the agency may conduct and factors such as complaints from clients.
- Consider conducting a broad-based survey of prebankruptcy credit counselors.
- Choose a few demonstrably effective indicators in developing a set of operational measures of effectiveness.
- Consider developing means to take into account debtors' characteristics in measuring the effectiveness of a credit-counseling agency.
- Consider which debtor characteristics ought to be taken into account in evaluating the performance of a counseling agency.

Acknowledgments

The authors would like to thank the bankruptcy study-group members (see the appendix for a list) for providing their insight on what constitutes effective credit counseling. We would also like to thank Susan Keating of the NFCC, David Jones of the Association of Independent Consumer Credit Counseling Organizations, and Mark Guimond of the American Association of Debt Management Organizations for participating in study-group discussions and sharing the experiences of their members. The insightful review comments by Mary Jo Wiggins, University of San Diego Law School; Roberto Quercia, University of North Carolina at Chapel Hill; and Matt Lewis of RAND improved the report immensely. We thank Linda Truitt of the National Institute of Justice for organizing and aptly managing the process.

Abbreviations

AADMO	American Association of Debt Management Organizations
BAPCPA	Bankruptcy Abuse Prevention and Consumer Protection Act of 2005
DMP	debt-management plan
EOUST	Executive Office for U.S. Trustees
GAO	U.S. Government Accountability Office
ISE	RAND Infrastructure, Safety, and Environment
MMI	Money Management International
NFCC	National Foundation for Credit Counseling
NIJ	National Institute of Justice
USTP	U.S. Trustee Program

CHAPTER ONE

Introduction

Background

The Bankruptcy Abuse Prevention and Consumer Protection Act of 2005 (BAPCPA) provided new requirements for bankruptcy filers and gave the U.S. Trustee Program (USTP) new areas of responsibility. One of the new requirements is that any individual who files for bankruptcy must have received credit counseling during the 180 days prior to filing. When a consumer completes such prebankruptcy credit counseling, he or she receives a certificate that must be submitted at the time of bankruptcy filing. USTP was charged with approving nonprofit agencies to provide this counseling service and with annually reapproving all such providers. Once a consumer has gone through bankruptcy, the new law also requires him or her to attend a debtor-education course.

BAPCPA requires that USTP approve or reapprove a credit-counseling agency only if it

> demonstrates that it will provide qualified counselors, maintain adequate provision for safe-keeping and payment of client funds, provide adequate counseling with respect to client credit problems, and deal responsibly and effectively with other matters relating to the quality, effectiveness, and financial security of the services it provides. (11 U.S.C. 111[c][1])

Accordingly, USTP is required to consider both the manner in which the counseling agency goes about counseling and the effectiveness of its services. In initially approving agencies to perform prebankruptcy credit counseling, USTP has focused on characteristics of the agency and its counselors. USTP's requirements for an agency wanting to become a provider of prebankruptcy credit counseling include the following (USTP, 2006):

- The agency must operate as a nonprofit with an independent governing board that does not directly benefit from outcomes of the counseling services.
- The agency must have responsible and effective business practices and, with some exceptions, have had at least two years of prior credit-counseling experience.
- The agency must provide adequate counseling that includes an assessment of the client's current financial condition and the reasons for the client's poor financial state. The counseling session will be 60 to 90 minutes in length and must include alternative ways of resolving the financial problems.
- The agency must charge reasonable fees and may not withhold counseling because of a client's inability to pay.
- Counselors must be accredited by a recognized, independent organization, such as the National Foundation for Credit Counseling (NFCC) or the Association of Independent

Consumer Credit Counseling Agencies, and must have at least six months of counseling experience.

- An agency that provides a debt-management plan must have adequate financial resources to provide services throughout the life of the plan and must keep adequate financial records.

USTP is now faced with having to decide whether to reapprove or remove agencies that are on the approved list of credit-counseling agencies. To do this, USTP must develop criteria for measuring the effectiveness of counseling-agency services that may be used to evaluate whether agencies qualify for approval or reapproval. USTP will have to decide whether to focus on a consumer's postcounseling decision to file for bankruptcy, alternatives to filing for bankruptcy, or some measure of the delivery of "enough" financial information such that consumers know their range of options.

For example, one might think that anyone who goes through prebankruptcy credit counseling and then chooses not to file for bankruptcy has received effective credit counseling. But it is likely that some—perhaps many—debtors' financial situations will have so deteriorated before they seek prebankruptcy credit counseling that bankruptcy is their only recourse. A recent U.S. Government Accountability Office (GAO) study reports that anecdotal evidence suggests just that: By the time debtors seek prebankruptcy credit counseling, their financial situation is dire enough to allow few alternatives to bankruptcy (GAO, 2007). There may even be cases in which a debtor's financial situation has so deteriorated that a bankruptcy filing is the best option, and yet, because of poor counseling, the debtor chooses not to file. However, no such scenario has been reported to USTP.

In such cases, effective credit counseling may equate with delivering sufficient financial information to provide the consumer with a range of options. A counseling session typically runs 60 to 90 minutes, and the counselor needs to spend a substantial portion of that time learning the details of the debtor's financial circumstances. There simply may not be enough time to improve the debtor's financial knowledge such that a different financial course can be chosen. The debtor may not be a voluntary participant and thus is in the counseling session only because it is a required condition of filing for bankruptcy. In contrast to predischarge debtor education, prebankruptcy credit counseling has more limited objectives. If the purpose of credit counseling is to improve the debtor's knowledge about the range of options available, the effectiveness of credit counseling might be defined in terms of a counseled debtor's financial knowledge.

Complicating the issue of effectiveness is the increased use of Internet-based credit counseling. NFCC has reported that the costs of providing counseling in the traditional delivery modes—in person or by phone—exceed the fees brought in for the counseling (NFCC, 2006b). Not surprisingly, several credit-counseling agencies have dramatically increased the use of the Internet to provide prebankruptcy credit counseling, since this is a less expensive method. This raises the question of whether the mode of delivery, particularly delivery through the Internet, affects the adequacy and effectiveness of the counseling provided.

The basic questions that the Executive Office for U.S. Trustees (EOUST), which manages USTP, is attempting to explore related to prebankruptcy credit counseling are as follows:

- What constitutes effective credit counseling in the prebankruptcy context?
- What are appropriate operational measures of effective prebankruptcy credit counseling?

- Does the mode of delivery of prebankruptcy credit counseling, particularly delivery through the Internet, influence the effectiveness of the counseling?

Objectives and Approach

USTP asked RAND for assistance in examining what constitutes effective prebankruptcy credit counseling and how it could be measured.

RAND's approach to meeting this objective consisted of reviewing the relevant literature that could inform the three questions and consulting with a bankruptcy study group of academic, government, and private-sector experts formed as part of a joint National Institute of Justice–USTP (NIJ-USTP) project to study bankruptcy fraud, abuse, and error to get feedback on the literature review results. (See the appendix for a list of study-group members.)

We reviewed the literature to assess the extent to which empirical research has identified operational measures of what makes a traditional credit-counseling program effective and the role of the various modes of delivery. We also reviewed the literature in related fields, such as financial-literacy programs and prepurchase homeownership counseling, for insight into what constitutes effective counseling in those contexts and whether effectiveness varies by mode of delivery.

With results from the review in hand and given the challenge of identifying operational measures of effective prebankruptcy credit counseling, we briefed those results to the bankruptcy study group at a meeting in February 2006 and received their feedback. Following additional literature review, we briefed the group again at a meeting in September 2006 that included representatives of three credit-counseling associations.[1]

Organization of This Report

The remainder of this report is organized as follows. We begin with a brief history of the credit-counseling industry to provide some context. The next chapter presents the results of our literature review. In light of what was learned from the research and from the suggestions based on discussions with the bankruptcy study group, we review, in the last chapter, the challenges facing USTP in assessing the effectiveness of both credit counseling and modes of delivery and offer suggestions for next steps.

The appendix contains a list of the members of the bankruptcy study group.

---

[1] At the September 2006 meeting, study-group members were given briefings on the prebankruptcy credit-counseling provision by USTP and by three credit counseling associations—NFCC, Association of Independent Consumer Credit Counseling Agencies, and American Association of Debt Management Organizations (AADMO).

CHAPTER TWO

Brief History of the Credit-Counseling Industry

In this chapter, we provide a brief history of the credit-counseling industry as context.

The industry of credit counseling began in the mid-1960s in an effort by creditor banks and credit-card companies to reduce a growing trend in personal bankruptcies (U.S. Senate, 2005). Historically, these were community-based, not-for-profit agencies with trained counselors who would meet with consumers who were deeply in debt (GAO, 2007). Typically, these meetings took place in person over multiple sessions. The counselor would analyze the consumer's income, expenses, and debt; discuss how he or she came to be in financial distress; and conduct budget planning to help keep the consumer out of financial trouble in the future (U.S. Senate, 2005).

One of the steps a counselor might recommend is for the consumer to go into a debt-management plan (DMP). With such a plan, the consumer makes a single monthly payment to the agency, and, in return, the agency distributes payments to creditors to pay off unsecured debts. The agency negotiates with creditors on the consumer's behalf for reduced interest rates and reduced monthly payments and to have certain fees waived, such as late fees. The credit-counseling agencies would receive a payment from the creditors to cover expenses such as salaries and operational costs. The share to the agency averaged between 12 and 15 percent of the payments received by creditors as a result of the DMP. Some agencies may have charged or requested additional nominal fees to cover their expenses related to managing the DMP (U.S. Senate, 2005).

The 1990s brought tremendous growth in credit-card debt, which also brought new providers into the credit-counseling industry. A 2005 Senate report on the changing credit-counseling industry noted that many of the new entrants were not community-based agencies that focused on in-person counseling sessions (U.S. Senate, 2005). Rather, these providers were nationwide, for-profit entities that interacted with consumers primarily through the Internet or telephone and were geared toward enrolling consumers in DMPs. As will be noted in the following chapter, few consumers participating in prebankruptcy credit counseling enter into DMPs.

A recent GAO study on the value of the prebankruptcy credit-counseling requirement makes the following assessment of the credit-counseling industry:

> The FTC and others have noted that many credit counseling agencies operate honestly and fairly and that these agencies are professional operations that provide valuable services to financially distressed consumers. However, starting in the 1990s, consumer complaints about selected segments of the credit counseling industry spurred congressional hearings and federal and state investigations into the activities of many credit counseling agencies. For example, over the past few years, the FTC has settled enforcement actions against sev-

eral of these agencies for alleged abusive practices, including steering consumers into debt management plans that provided financial benefits to the agency but not to the consumer. Further, as part of its Credit Counseling Compliance Project, IRS has undertaken a broad examination effort of credit counseling organizations for compliance with the Internal Revenue Code, including the propriety of the organizations' tax-exempt status. Between January 2005 and March 2007, IRS had revoked or terminated the federal tax-exempt status of 19 credit counseling agencies, and as of March 2007, IRS had proposed revocations for an additional 28 agencies. (GAO, 2007, pp. 8–9)

CHAPTER THREE

Review of the Research

As noted previously, we reviewed the relevant literature to assess the extent to which empirical research has identified operational measures of what makes a traditional credit-counseling program effective and the role of the various modes of delivery. We also reviewed the literature in related fields, such as financial-literacy programs and prepurchase homeownership counseling, for insight into what constitutes effective counseling in those contexts and whether effectiveness varies by mode of delivery. This chapter presents the results of that review in terms of these areas.

Review of Credit-Counseling Literature

The counseling sessions for prebankruptcy clients appear to be similar to those for traditional credit-counseling clients, in which specific information about the consumer's income, debt, and expenses is assessed; a budget is developed; and the consumer and counselor discuss methods of avoiding financial trouble in the future. The counselor may obtain some information from the client's credit report; other information may be self-reported. When the session takes place via the Internet, the client typically logs on to the agency's Web site and inputs financial information similar to what would be provided during a phone or in-person session (GAO, 2007). Some Internet sessions are combined with a phone call with the counselor.

Little empirical research has been done on the issue of effective credit counseling or the effectiveness of various modes of delivery of credit counseling. Here, we discuss what is available, starting with a review of an NFCC survey on prebankruptcy credit counseling.

NFCC is an association of credit-counseling agencies. It conducted a survey of 107 of its member agencies to assess the status of the provision of the newly required prebankruptcy credit-counseling session (NFCC, 2006b).[1] The survey covered the period of October 17, 2005, through August 31, 2006, the first almost 11 months of the new law. The numbers reported are noteworthy, because almost 70 percent of the approved credit-counseling agencies are NFCC members (NFCC, 2006a).

The members surveyed reported providing 436,937 prebankruptcy filing sessions over that same period and issued 485,963 prefiling certificates. The number of certificates exceeds the number of sessions due to spouses attending jointly and group sessions, but each individual who completes the session receives an individual certificate. Even when filing for bank-

---

[1] NFCC has 115 member agencies. One hundred eight have been EOUST-approved to offer prebankruptcy credit counseling; 107 of the EOUST-approved agencies participated in the survey.

ruptcy as a married couple, each spouse receives a certificate by law. These certificates must be obtained prior to filing for bankruptcy. Approximately 385,000 bankruptcy filings were made during the same period. The discrepancy in numbers may stem from several factors. Some of the people who received counseling may have decided not to file for bankruptcy. Others may have intended to file but had not yet done so at the time of the survey (given that there is a 180-day window allowed between counseling and filing).

According to the NFCC survey, prebankruptcy credit counseling appears quite different from traditional credit counseling in both debt levels involved and mode of delivery. In terms of the former, the survey revealed that those seeking prebankruptcy credit counseling had an average income of $26,873 and held unsecured debt averaging $38,472. This means that average unsecured debts exceeded average annual income by $11,599 for these clients. For those seeking regular credit counseling (nonbankruptcy), the reverse is true. The average income of those seeking regular credit counseling was $31,143, with average unsecured debt of $22,597. The report comments that, by the time most of these debtors seek prebankruptcy credit counseling, their debts far outstrip their income, which often results in bankruptcy being the best option. The prime reasons cited for clients finding themselves facing bankruptcy were poor money management (66 percent) and loss of income (29 percent).

The mode of delivery for prebankruptcy credit counseling is far more heavily weighted toward phone and online counseling than is the mode of delivery for traditional credit counseling. The survey revealed that, during the first 11 months of the new prebankruptcy credit-counseling requirement, 61 percent of sessions took place over the telephone, 24 percent took place through the Internet, and 15 percent took place in person. A GAO study reports that, between July and October 2006, 45 percent of counseling sessions took place over the phone, 45 percent took place through the Internet, and 13 percent took place in person.[2] The NFCC survey notes the contrast between these numbers and those for traditional financial counseling, in which 45 percent of the sessions take place over the telephone, 36 percent take place in person, and 19 percent via the Internet.[3] This shift was quite a surprise to most people in the credit-counseling industry. Just six weeks prior to BAPCPA taking effect, NFCC members forecast that about half of prebankruptcy credit counseling would take place in person and 10 percent over the telephone (NFCC, 2006a).

This shift toward distance counseling (by phone and online) does allow agencies to provide counseling services to those in more geographically remote places who may not have physical access to certified financial counselors. Distance counseling provides an opportunity for agencies to expand their base of bankruptcy clients, though the availability of such service would be limited to those with an Internet connection and some technological knowledge. The shift may also reflect a movement toward the less expensive counseling modes. NFCC estimates that the cost of a face-to-face counseling session is $54.92, of a phone counseling session is $52.47, and of an Internet counseling session is $44.91. NFCC agencies noted a widening gap between fees received from clients and the cost of service delivery, with a reported 16 percent of fees being waived due to clients' inability to pay. Agencies approved to provide

---

[2]   The numbers came from USTP data collected from certificates issued between July 11, 2006, and October 17, 2006 (GAO, 2007, p. 21). These data are likely to change as reporting becomes more consistent.

[3]   At the second meeting of the bankruptcy study group, Mark Guimond of AADMO reported that, of the prebankruptcy credit-counseling sessions provided by AADMO agencies, 50 percent were in person, 40 percent were by phone, and 10 percent were via the Internet (Guimond, 2006).

prebankruptcy credit counseling must not turn away any clients due to an inability to pay. This shift toward less expensive methods of delivery can be expected to increase if the cost-revenue gap continues to widen.

The NFCC report recognized the need for better methods of assessing whether credit counseling has been effective (NFCC, 2006b). Some of the NFCC agencies administered pre- and postcounseling tests to assess knowledge gains and report positive findings.[4] However, they are not sure whether good test results indicate improved financial knowledge and behavioral changes or rather just reflect short-term retention of the information. As a result, NFCC has formed an Outcomes and Impact Task Force that will develop performance metrics for its financial-counseling and -education services (not just prebankruptcy credit counseling). The metrics will be geared toward assessing behavioral change, increased knowledge, and changes in attitude among its clients.

GAO (2007) examined materials from 15 approved credit-counseling providers that accounted for more than two-thirds of the prebankruptcy credit-counseling certificates that were issued between January 9, 2006, and October 17, 2006. The materials they examined included counselor-training manuals, disclosures, curricula, workbooks, and handouts. They concluded that all methods of delivery (in-person, phone, or Internet) generally provided the same content and structure within the counseling session (GAO, 2007). They did not address the issue of whether the effectiveness of any given content or structure was independent of mode of delivery.

A recent study by Staten and Barron (2006) analyzed credit records of approximately 60,000 clients two years after their credit-counseling sessions. They identified four outcome measures of whether credit counseling was effective. Two of the measures are indicators of credit worthiness (bankruptcy-risk score and new account delinquency risk score). The other two measures are more specific indicators of credit use (total nonmortgage balances and number of accounts in delinquency).

Staten and Barron (2006) looked at traditional credit counseling, not prebankruptcy credit counseling. Their research analyzed two modes of delivery—telephone and in-person. They noted that clients who sought in-person counseling perceived their financial situation as more serious than did those who sought telephone counseling. Those who perceived their financial problems as severe were self-selecting into in-person sessions. The authors also found that consumers receiving in-person counseling were likelier to file for bankruptcy in the two years following the session. However, because of the self-selection, we cannot discern whether this was the result of their severer financial condition or of in-person credit counseling being less effective.

Staten and Barron (2006) also found that the credit counseling's mode of delivery appeared to have no impact on a client's creditworthiness two years after the session, nor did it affect total nonmortgage balances two years later. They did find fewer delinquent accounts among those who received in-person counseling than among those who received telephone counseling. The authors suggest that it might be useful to augment their research with more subjective measures of consumer-credit performance, such as surveys of consumer attitudes, financial knowledge pre- and postcounseling, and perceived financial stress pre- and postcounseling.

---

[4] The report does not cite how many agencies administered such tests nor whether these methods are being studied empirically.

Staten and Barron will be conducting a second phase of this work that includes alternative performance measures for assessing counseling's impact on borrowers and analyses of whether certain types of debtors benefit more from one delivery method than another.

Visa USA (1999) conducted a survey of individuals who sought credit-counseling services. Included in this survey were individuals who completed DMPs and individuals who dropped out of DMPs. One of the findings was that almost half the individuals who sought credit counseling struggled for more than a year before seeking financial help. This suggests that a significant fraction of those who participate in credit counseling may already be on the verge of bankruptcy. Therefore, filing for bankruptcy after participating in a credit-counseling session may not be a good indicator of whether that counseling session was or was not effective, since filing for bankruptcy may indeed be the best option.

Review of Other, Related Literature

Since there is little research on credit counseling specifically or on the modes of service delivery related to credit counseling, we also reviewed research in related areas.

Literature on the Effectiveness of Online Instruction

There is particular concern about the effectiveness of online counseling, which has been on the rise in the prebankruptcy credit-counseling context, when reviewing the NFCC studies (2006a, 2006b). Although there is little research on online service delivery related to credit counseling, there is a rich body of literature on the effectiveness of online instruction in higher education and training courses.

There are basically two schools of thought on the effectiveness of online instruction relative to classroom instruction. The first position argues that the delivery medium (computers, video teleconferencing, the Internet) is not as important as the instructional method—that is, the technique used to convey course content, such as lectures, textbooks, discussions, and group assignments (Clark, 1983, 1994; Sitzmann et al., 2006). This position has received broad support, but dissenters abound. The second position argues that online instruction is more effective because it offers greater flexibility and access to more instructional methods rather than only one instructional method (Dumont, 1996; Hiltz and Wellman, 1997; Sullivan, 2001).

There is research supporting both of these positions, as well as research that argues that they perform equally well (Russell, 1999). There does not appear to be consensus on which method is more effective. Effectiveness often depends on the specific course or training, what the person is being asked to learn, and how the knowledge is then used. There are also blended learning programs that provide some combination of traditional and online instruction (e.g., classroom instruction, online chat rooms, posted lecture notes). This method has gained popularity but has yet to be well studied. We heard from the credit-counseling associations that this blended approach is often used in providing prebankruptcy counseling. Debtors may participate in an online session and then have a phone follow-up with a counselor.

We think that this body of research has little transferable value to the issue of the relative effectiveness of online prebankruptcy credit counseling for at least three reasons. First, most of the courses studied were semester-long courses that included repeated interaction between the same individuals, thereby providing time for students to get accustomed to the online nature of the instruction and allowing instructors numerous opportunities to assess whether the students were absorbing the material and to make adjustments accordingly. In contrast, online prebankruptcy credit counseling has to get the message across in one session of 60 to 90 minutes.

Second, many of the assessments of the effectiveness of online instruction in higher education compare online courses to traditional classroom courses. For online credit counseling, a better comparison would be between online instruction and traditional, in-person counseling, or perhaps between online instruction and phone counseling, which is second in frequency to in-person credit counseling.

Third, university students are, on average, more technologically sophisticated than are most consumers who are seeking prebankruptcy credit counseling. Similarly, university students are likelier than most such consumers to have personal computers and access to an Internet connection.

Literature on the Effectiveness of Online Training Courses of Shorter Duration

We also examined the literature on online training courses of shorter duration. These are often used in organizations to provide just-in-time training—that is, training when and where the employee needs it. Examples of this type of training are sales training, mandatory training on company policies and procedures, training for a new data platform, and training on a new product line. These types of online training offer a better comparison to the prebankruptcy credit-counseling session offered online, primarily because the training addresses a specific topic and is delivered in a similar length of time (60 to 90 minutes). There is little good empirical research on the effectiveness of these training courses. Most studies are originated by, or use the experiences of, companies that have an interest in promoting online training (Kathawala and Wilgen, 2004). These training courses have been found to be cost-effective because they eliminate or reduce travel costs, travel time, and instructor pay. Measuring whether they have been effective is more complicated.

These online learning systems are often provided with a built-in assessment function that automatically tracks enrollments, completion rates, progress, pre- and postlearning test scores, and certifications (Weekes, 2006). These variables are useful but do not necessarily measure whether the training has been effective, and there is no real consensus on how to go about measuring effectiveness (Weekes, 2006). Forrester Research, an independent research firm, polled training managers at Global 2,500 companies about obstacles to online learning. The three most common obstacles cited were lack of interactivity (56 percent), cultural resistance (41 percent), and lack of bandwidth (36 percent) (Dalton et al., 2000).

Literature on Financial-Literacy Training

We also reviewed the literature on financial-literacy training for any accepted standards related to appropriate measures of effectiveness of sessions and the relative effectiveness of alternative modes of service delivery. A review by Braunstein and Welch (2002) of the Federal Reserve Board on the issue of financial-literacy practices concluded that, overall, the evidence suggests that financial education can result in better-informed consumers who make better financial decisions. They acknowledge that the findings of studies of the effectiveness of financial-literacy training have been mixed. Some of these programs have been successful at affecting discrete aspects of a person's financial state, such as maintaining a mortgage, increasing savings, or participating in an employer-sponsored benefit plan. The studies show that having more financial information does not necessarily result in improved financial behavior. The authors recognize that defining and quantifying what makes a successful financial-literacy program remain a challenge, since little research has been conducted in this area. They go on to suggest that the development of consistent standards for measuring results, which currently do not exist, could increase the success of financial-literacy programs. But they also recognize that those standards will vary depending on the focus of the program (general financial-literacy programs versus programs focused on areas such as homeownership counseling).[5]

A study by Zhan, Anderson, and Scott (2006) evaluated the financial knowledge of 168 low-income individuals enrolled in a financial-education program by administering pre- and post-training tests. On average, participants correctly answered 54 percent of the questions on the pretraining test and 74 percent on the post-training test. This indicates that the program was effective in improving financial knowledge. The authors recognized that improving financial knowledge does not prove that the ultimate goal of positively influencing financial behavior was achieved. They suggested that follow-up surveys would need to be conducted to test whether the knowledge gains persisted and whether financial behavior changed as a result.

An interesting feature of the Zhan, Anderson, and Scott (2006) study was that it also collected information on participants' background characteristics to examine how they related to financial-knowledge levels or affected program outcomes. They collected variables on demographics (gender, age, race or ethnicity, marital status, and number of children in household), education (education level and English proficiency), and economics (household income, employment status, assets, and debts) and compared them to the pre- and post-training test scores. They found that pretraining knowledge varied depending on participant characteristics; for example, married participants and those whose primary language was English had higher pretraining test scores. In terms of post-training test scores, education levels, English proficiency, race or ethnicity, and marital status significantly affected financial-knowledge gains and therefore program outcomes. This would suggest that such financial-literacy training programs would be more effective if they were tailored to meet the varying needs of low-income individuals.

Literature on the Effectiveness of Prepurchase Homeownership Counseling

Finally, we reviewed the literature on the effectiveness of prepurchase homeownership counseling. The effectiveness of this type of counseling is typically measured by loan performance (e.g., 30 days or 60 days delinquent) or by default rates (often defined as 90 days delinquent).

Hornburg (2004) reviewed the recent research literature on homeownership education and counseling. He concluded that "we do not know what approaches work best and for whom." This conclusion largely reflects the limits of the available data. Because the data are so limited, research simply has not had an opportunity to explore the effects of counseling. At the time of that study, Hornburg noted that only one published study, Hirad and Zorn (2001), presents credible and rigorous findings of the effects of homeownership counseling on borrowers' loan performance.

Hirad and Zorn (2001) studied the effect of prepurchase homeownership counseling on 90-day delinquency rates. Their study assessed data on almost 40,000 mortgages origi-

---

[5]   The Federal Reserve Board confirmed that it has not updated this 2002 review of financial-literacy practices. In addition, it is not aware of any studies that attempt to assess the effectiveness of various modes of delivery of financial-literacy programs (Hogarth, 2006).

nated under a special lending program (Freddie Mac® Affordable Gold®).[6] Most borrowers in the study were required to receive homeownership counseling as a condition of their mortgage, although some borrowers were exempt from the requirement based on their perceived lower risk. The exempt mortgages served as a quasicontrol group of borrowers who received no counseling.

The study found that the 90-day delinquency rate was 19 percent lower for borrowers who received prepurchase homeownership counseling than it was for those who did not receive it. The study also compared the 90-day delinquency rate of borrowers receiving the counseling through different delivery methods. Borrowers who received individual counseling had a 34-percent reduction in delinquency rates, all other things being equal. Borrowers who received classroom counseling had a 26-percent reduction in delinquency rates, and those who participated in home-study counseling (usually through workbooks) had a 21-percent reduction. The study found no statistically significant reduction in delinquency rates for borrowers participating in telephone counseling.

A recent study by Quercia and Spader (2007) notes that, although there was a dramatic boom in prepurchase homeownership counseling programs in the 1990s and into the 2000s, there has been little formal evaluation of the counseling process. This is partly attributable to a lack of agreed-upon standards and wide variation in curriculum, format, and provider types, all of which make formal analysis difficult. The result is a lack of clear consensus about the effectiveness of prepurchase homeownership counseling, regardless of the form of delivery.

Quercia and Spader's (2007) research used a data set of 2,688 affordable mortgage borrowers from the Community Advantage Program, of whom almost 10 percent defaulted and about 53 percent refinanced. A major advantage of this data source is that borrowers participate in a range of prepurchase homeownership-counseling programs offered by different providers. The sample included borrowers who received some form of homeownership education and counseling (43 percent) and borrowers who received none. Of those who completed some form of counseling, about 80 percent were required by the lender to participate in such a program.

Quercia and Spader (2007) found that the type of counseling program suggests different levels of program intensity. Individual counseling and classroom instruction are substantially more intensive than telephone counseling or home study. The number of hours invested by program participants ranged from 9.8 hours in individual counseling, 6.8 hours in classroom instruction, 2.9 hours for home study, and 0.7 hours for telephone counseling.

Using these intensities, they separated borrowers who had received homeownership education and counseling into two groups based on the relative intensities of the programs: (1) those who participated through individual counseling or classroom instruction and (2) those who participated over the telephone or through home study. They then estimated the impact of each type of counseling on refinancing and default using a competing-risks model. They conclude that counseling programs based on individual counseling or classroom instruction improve a borrower's decision about refinancing but that programs based on telephone or home-study counseling did not affect borrower behavior. Counseling had no apparent effect on default.

---

[6]   The U.S. Congress created Freddie Mac to work with mortgage lenders to help people get lower housing costs and better access to home financing.

This literature does not offer many useful lessons for prebankruptcy credit counseling. It is focused on homeowners' loan performance. However appropriate this focus might be for improving understanding of how counseling might assist potential homeowners, it does not illuminate measures of effectiveness for prebankruptcy counseling. Further, the research largely addresses the question of whether homeownership counseling has an effect. While this question is important in the homeownership context, it is irrelevant in the prebankruptcy-counseling context. Congress has determined that prebankruptcy counseling is required. The relevant question for EOUST is how to best fulfill that mandate. Finally, a large and rapidly growing share of prebankruptcy counseling is being provided over the Internet. Consequently, EOUST must address the questions of how mode of delivery influences the effectiveness of prebankruptcy counseling and whether and how content and structure should be modified by mode of delivery.

CHAPTER FOUR

Conclusions and Recommendations

In this chapter, we present some conclusions and recommendations based both on the comments and suggestions made by study-group participants and on our own independent research. The study-group members were not asked to approve these recommendations.

Conclusions

USTP faces challenges in assessing the adequacy and effectiveness of its approved prebankruptcy credit-counseling providers. USTP's three main questions related to prebankruptcy credit counseling remain: What constitutes effective credit counseling in the prebankruptcy context? What are appropriate operational measures of effective prebankruptcy credit counseling? Does the mode of delivery of prebankruptcy credit counseling, particularly the delivery of counseling via the Internet, influence the adequacy and effectiveness of the counseling? This report documents USTP's due diligence in investigating whether standards or protocols exist for measuring effectiveness in the world of credit counseling and other related fields.

To address these questions and to eventually develop operational measures of effectiveness, we conclude that **USTP's first step should be to identify the goals of prebankruptcy credit counseling. The other suggestions depend on the goals being explicitly defined.**

Even if goals are defined, we conclude that **there are no common standards or accepted sets of metrics for USTP to adopt in whole as it attempts to assess the prebankruptcy credit-counseling agencies, but there may be many transferable pieces from some of the research studies reviewed.** Although many of the approaches had similarities, every field approached the assessment of effectiveness somewhat differently based on its specific goals.

We also conclude that **there is no universally accepted view on the effectiveness of mode of delivery** and that **there is no single most effective mode of delivery. The research shows that the effectiveness of the modes seems to vary depending on the type of counseling being delivered and its purpose.** More specifically, we found no empirical research on the effectiveness of Internet delivery of prebankruptcy credit counseling, nor did we discover relevant studies from the fields of credit counseling, financial literacy, or prepurchase homeownership counseling. Most of the available research studies relating to delivery of information through the Internet are predominantly geared toward higher education, and we conclude that this research has little transferable value. Additionally, we did not come across instances in which this delivery method was used to handle specific personal information. Whether an online session alone, which, by its nature, is somewhat standardized, can effectively take into account an individual's specific financial situation and all its nuances is questionable. The blended programs in which online sessions are paired with telephone calls with actual counselors could be effective, but the method should be studied further.

We now briefly summarize the research findings underlying these general conclusions surrounding the three questions.

Goals

The goals of prebankruptcy credit counseling need to be clarified. Before one can measure whether prebankruptcy credit counseling is effective, the goals of prebankruptcy credit counseling must be explicitly identified. Once the goals are explicit, operational measures of effectiveness can be developed against which approved credit-counseling agencies can be measured. Broader goals of the credit-counseling industry at large, such as improved financial literacy, are too general for this context. The statute does not require that the counseling session result in a behavioral change by the debtor, such as an improved credit score after the counseling session. We think that it is reasonable to assume that congressional intent was that the debtor be made aware, prior to filing for bankruptcy, of the range of options and the associated risks based on the debtor's particular financial situation.

Measures of Effectiveness

The literature provides a confusing message about the effectiveness of financial counseling. Staten and Barron (2006) found that the decision to voluntarily seek credit counseling was a strong indicator of subsequent credit problems. The survey by Visa USA (1999) also suggests that individuals who seek credit counseling likely struggle for some time before seeking financial help. This suggests that a significant fraction of those who participate in credit counseling may already be on the verge of bankruptcy. Therefore, filing for bankruptcy after having participated in a credit-counseling session may not be a good indicator of whether or not that counseling session was effective.

Braunstein and Welch's (2002) review of financial-literacy training found that consumers receiving financial training can make better financial decisions but do not always do so. Similarly, the study by Zhan, Anderson, and Scott (2006) on financial-literacy training for low-income individuals found that such training did improve financial knowledge in the short term. The authors acknowledge that whether these knowledge gains persist over time or influence behavior is not known and has not been studied. Because of this lack of research on behavioral changes, defining what constitutes a successful financial-training program is still a challenge, and consistent standards for measuring results do not exist.

Hirad and Zorn (2001) report that delinquency rates were 19 percent lower for borrowers receiving prepurchase homeownership counseling than for borrowers who did not seek counseling. In sum, a standard definition of *effective counseling* does not exist, even within issue areas (financial-literacy training, credit counseling, or prepurchase homeownership counseling) and certainly not across issue areas.

Metrics

The professionals confirm that there is no silver bullet when it comes to metrics. Representatives from three primary credit-counseling associations were asked to offer insight into this issue of metrics of effective credit counseling.[1] When pressed on the issue of what constitutes effective credit counseling, they all recognized that the development of specific metrics will be difficult. Traditional measures of increased financial literacy are improved credit scores and success at completing DMPs. Neither was thought to be immediately useful in the prebankruptcy context. Both of these are metrics of longer-term behavioral changes and can be tracked only through a longitudinal research study. Additionally, it appears that very few of those seeking prebankruptcy credit counseling are opting for DMPs—less than 4 percent, according to the NFCC (2006b). The general objective of credit-counseling associations is to provide the individual with enough information to make an informed decision about his or her financial future, but there are no metrics for evaluating whether this is being done effectively. Currently, the credit-counseling associations rely on training and third-party accreditation of the counselors and agencies as proxies for effectiveness.

Mode of Delivery

The literature generally, but not always, suggests that in-person counseling is more effective than other modes of delivery. Staten and Barron (2006) found that the mode of delivery (telephone or in person) of credit counseling had no impact on a client's creditworthiness. They did note, however, that those receiving in-person counseling had fewer delinquent accounts, one of the four factors they measured. Hirad and Zorn (2001) found that receiving individual counseling reduced delinquency rates by 34 percent; receiving classroom counseling reduced delinquency rates by 26 percent; receiving home study reduced them by 21 percent; and receiving telephone counseling made no reduction in delinquency rates, which could indicate a self-selection bias. Quercia and Spader (2007) found that homeownership-counseling programs based on individual counseling or classroom instruction improve a borrower's decision about refinancing but that programs based on telephone or home-study counseling did not affect borrower behavior.

Internet counseling in this context, or even in a relevant related field, has not been empirically studied. We found no research that assessed the effectiveness of Internet credit counseling. In fact, most of the research reviewed (including recently published research) did not include Internet delivery as one of the modes evaluated. Although delivery of credit counseling through the Internet may have been available for several years, the spike in use of the Internet for credit counseling seems to be a product of BAPCPA and has not yet been well studied.

Regarding the effectiveness of various modes of delivery, there was clearly some uneasiness expressed at the study-group meeting about relying solely on an Internet session for prebankruptcy credit counseling. Some felt that Internet counseling alone is insufficient and that it should be coupled with a phone or in-person session so that the counseling is personalized. Everyone's financial situation is different, and counseling must be tailored to the specific needs of the individual to have a hope of being effective. The credit-counseling associations noted that the prebankruptcy credit-counseling sessions are being offered at a financial loss to many

---

[1] Representatives from NFCC, Association of Independent Consumer Credit Counseling Agencies, and AADMO were asked to make a brief presentation at the second study-group meeting and to participate in the discussion. They were asked to address specifically this issue of metrics for evaluating effective credit counseling and the effectiveness of various modes of delivery.

of the agencies. This has led to the increased use of phone and Internet counseling sessions, both of which are less expensive to provide than in-person sessions.

There was also concern about verifying that the person who engages in the online session is actually the debtor. The provisions of BAPCPA related to application procedures and criteria for approval of nonprofit credit-counseling agencies require that verification procedures be in place.[2] Some providers require a signed affidavit before they will assign a login and password for the online session. Money Management International (MMI) provides one example of how agencies verify online identity. MMI operates prebankruptcy credit-counseling agencies across the country; it uses information from a counselee's credit report to pose questions that someone other than the counselee may have a hard time answering. This happens during the part of the online session that is interactive between the counselor and counselee, during which specific financial information is being collected. We are not aware of any empirical studies or published observations of verification procedures of Internet credit counseling. NFCC, whose members constitute the bulk of prebankruptcy credit-counseling providers, states that it has deferred to the verification innovation of its members, subject to the approval of the EOUST, and has not collected data to support or to recommend an industry standard on this issue.

Recommendations

Given these conclusions, USTP must make its way where no clear path exists. As such, we offer the following recommendations.

Use Upcoming Reviews and Reports to Inform the Process of Moving Forward

USTP should use a series of upcoming reviews and reports to help it inform the process of developing operational measures of effectiveness and approving or reapproving credit-counseling agencies.

- USTP is currently conducting quality service reviews, which are basically field reviews of some of the approved credit-counseling agencies. USTP can use the quality service reviews as an opportunity to gather candidate indicators of effective prebankruptcy credit counseling. As USTP talks to credit-counseling providers, it could probe about indicators capable of demonstrating that the counseling has been effective in the prebankruptcy context. These experienced counselors will likely also have thoughts on the appropriateness of the modes of delivery. USTP can also review the verification procedures of those agencies providing Internet credit counseling.
- Staten and Barron are working on phase two of their research, which will more specifically examine whether certain types of debtors benefit more from one type of delivery mode than from another. This will be empirical research that may lend insight into operational measures of prebankruptcy credit counseling.

---

[2]   From the Code of Federal Regulations:

> If an agency offers telephone or Internet credit counseling services, the agency must, in addition to all other requirements, demonstrate sufficient experience and proficiency in designing and providing such services over the telephone and/or Internet, including the verification procedures to identify the person receiving the counseling services and to ensure that the counseling services are properly completed. (28 CFR 58.15[f][3][ii])

- NFCC has assembled an Outcomes and Impact Task Force to develop performance metrics to assess effectiveness of its counseling and education services. The criteria will address both credit-counseling and debtor-education services. The resulting report is expected sometime in 2007.

Consider Other Options to Move Forward While Awaiting Results of Upcoming Events

There are other suggestions that USTP may want to consider as it contemplates reapproving providers and develops a process for constructing operational measures of effectiveness. These suggestions, which stem from discussions at the study-group meeting and are expanded in this report, are as follows:

- USTP's process for evaluating prebankruptcy credit-counseling agencies should evolve over time as more becomes known and more results come in from ongoing and future research. In the interim, USTP is still required to approve and reapprove agencies to provide the prebankruptcy credit-counseling service. USTP's process for initially approving credit-counseling agencies appears to be thorough and, at this point, can rely only on indirect factors such as accreditation and training requirements. In reapproving agencies, USTP should also look at whether an agency is providing the services stated in its application to become an approved credit-counseling agency (e.g., covering certain types of material, methods of delivery, adequate verification procedures for Internet counseling). USTP can also consider any pre- and post-testing that the agency may conduct and factors such as complaints from clients.
- USTP may want to consider conducting a broad-scale survey of prebankruptcy credit counselors. USTP should attempt to capture these practitioners' views, based on their experiences, of what constitutes effective credit counseling for individuals on the verge of bankruptcy. A person in financial difficulty who seeks traditional credit counseling is in a different financial state from that of a person on the verge of bankruptcy who has likely been in financial difficulty for an extended period. The expectations of what constitutes effective credit counseling in a prebankruptcy context should be commensurate with what is feasible, given the debtor's current financial state.
- In developing a set of operational measures of effectiveness, USTP should keep it simple by choosing a few demonstrably effective indicators. A few of the indicators discussed at the study-group meeting were pre- and postcounseling literacy tests and a longitudinal study to track individuals' financial health over time. Other indicators could include an evaluation of the content of the counseling materials, an assessment of the counseling skills (perhaps via reviews by counselees), and any complaints received about a counselor or an agency.
- USTP should consider developing means for taking into account debtors' characteristics in measuring the effectiveness of a credit-counseling agency. In research, this is a technique called *case-mix adjustment*. There are likely to be significant variations among debtors in terms of both their financial circumstances and their backgrounds. It seems likely that it would be easier for counselors to achieve goals that demonstrate effectiveness when working with certain kinds of debtors or with debtors in certain kinds of financial positions. An agency that, by chance or design, happens to work with debtors in particularly difficult circumstances (e.g., an agency that is in an economically depressed area) is likely to appear less effective, even though it may, in fact, be doing a particularly effective

job given the debtors it is serving. The study by Zhan, Anderson, and Scott (2006) on financial-literacy training for low-income individuals shows that participants' background characteristics (education level, English proficiency, race or ethnicity, and marital status) significantly influence their knowledge gains and therefore program outcomes.

- The question of which debtor characteristics ought to be taken into account in evaluating the performance of a counseling agency needs to be considered—particularly those characteristics related to the extent to which counseling improved the debtors' knowledge of the range of options associated with their particular financial situation. For example, a debtor's education might be related to his or her ability to develop financial knowledge in counseling. More highly educated debtors might be better able to understand the intricacies of financial issues presented by a counselor. The circumstances that led to a debtor's decision to consider filing for bankruptcy might be important in evaluating the extent to which counseling affected the debtor's future behavior. Debtors driven to bankruptcy by an unanticipated financial blow might exhibit more consistent financial behavior than may debtors who generally live above their means.

Study-Group Members

Melyssa R. Barrett
Director, Loss Mitigation Products
Visa USA

James W. Boyd
Zimmerman, Kuhn, Darling, Boyd, Taylor
and Quandt

David L. Cotton
Managing partner
Cotton and Company

Ramona D. Elliott
Counsel for Bankruptcy Redress
Federal Trade Commission

Samuel J. Gerdano
Executive director
American Bankruptcy Institute

The Honorable Kevin R. Huennekens
Judge
U.S. Bankruptcy Court for the Eastern
District of Virginia

Barbara Kent, president
Coalition for Debtor Education

The Honorable Daniel R. Levinson
Inspector general
U.S. Department of Health and Human
Services

James Madden, special agent
Criminal Investigations
Internal Revenue Service

The Honorable Brian Miller
Inspector general
U.S. General Services Administration

Sybil Smith, senior analyst
Financial Crimes
Internal Revenue Service

The Honorable Roger M. Whelan
Bankruptcy judge, retired

Todd H. Zywicki
George Mason University School of Law

References

Braunstein, Sandra, and Carolyn Welch, "Financial Literacy: An Overview of Practice, Research, and Policy," *Federal Reserve Bulletin*, November 2002, pp. 445–457. As of July 6, 2007:
http://www.federalreserve.gov/pubs/bulletin/2002/1102lead.pdf

Clark, Richard E., "Reconsidering Research on Learning from Media," *Review of Educational Research*, Vol. 53, No. 4, Winter 1983, pp. 445–459.

———, "Media Will Never Influence Learning," *Educational Technology Research and Development*, Vol. 42, 1994, pp. 21–29.

Code of Federal Regulations, Part 58, Section 15, Qualifications for Approval as a Nonprofit Budget and Credit Counseling Agency, *Federal Register*, Vol. 71, No. 128, July 5, 2006, pp. 38078–38080. As of July 6, 2007:
http://www.usdoj.gov/olp/pdf/rin_1105-ab17.pdf

Dalton, John P., Harley Manning, Paul R. Hagen, Yolanda Paul, and Joyce Tong, *Online Training Needs a New Course*, Cambridge, Mass.: Forrester Research, August 2000.

Dumont, R. A., "Teaching and Learning in Cyberspace," *IEEE Transactions on Professional Communication*, Vol. 39, No. 4, December 1996, pp. 192–204.

GAO—*see* U.S. Government Accountability Office.

Guimond, Mark, "Presentation of the American Association of Debt Management Organizations to the Bankruptcy Study Group," Washington, D.C., September 2006.

Hiltz, Starr Roxanne, and Barry Wellman, "Asynchronous Learning Networks as a Virtual Classroom," *Communications of the ACM*, Vol. 40, No. 9, September 1997, pp. 44–49.

Hirad, Abdighani, and Peter M. Zorn, *A Little Knowledge Is a Good Thing: Empirical Evidence of the Effectiveness of Pre-Purchase Homeownership Counseling*, Cambridge, Mass.: Joint Center for Housing Studies of Harvard University, May 2001.

Hogarth, Jeanne, Federal Reserve Board, telephone conversation with Noreen Clancy, November 2006.

Hornburg, Steven P., *Strengthening the Case for Homeownership Counseling: Moving Beyond "a Little Bit of Knowledge,"* Cambridge, Mass.: Joint Center for Housing Studies, Graduate School of Design and John F. Kennedy School of Government, Harvard University, W04-12, 2004.

Kathawala, Yunus, and Andreas Wilgen, "E-Learning: Evaluation from an Organization's Perspective," *Training and Management Development Methods*, Vol. 18, No. 4, 2004, pp. 5.01–5.13.

National Foundation for Credit Counseling, *Meeting the Mandate: Consumer Counseling and Education Under the Bankruptcy Abuse Prevention and Consumer Protection Act, A Six Month Progress Report,* Silver Spring, Md.: NFCC, April 2006a. As of July 6, 2007:
http://www.nfcc.org/Newsroom/NFCC%206%20month%20report%20FINAL.pdf

———, *Consumer Counseling and Education Under BAPCPA: The Bankruptcy Abuse Prevention and Consumer Protection Act of 2005, Year One Report,* Silver Spring, Md.: NFCC, October 16, 2006b. As of July 6, 2007:
http://www.nfcc.org/NFCC_Year_One_Bankruptcy_Report2.pdf

NFCC—*see* National Foundation for Credit Counseling.

Quercia, Roberto G., and Jonathan S. Spader, *Does Homeownership Counseling Affect the Prepayment and Default Behavior of Affordable Mortgage Borrowers?* Chapel Hill, N.C.: Center for Community Capitalism, The Frank Hawkins Kenan Institute of Private Enterprise, University of North Carolina at Chapel Hill, May 2007.

Russell, Thomas L., *The No Significant Difference Phenomenon: As Reported in 355 Research Reports, Summaries, and Papers*, 5th ed., Raleigh, N.C.: North Carolina State University, 1999.

Sitzmann, Traci, Kurt Kraiger, David Stewart, and Robert Wisher, "The Comparative Effectiveness of Web-Based and Classroom Instruction: A Meta-Analysis," *Personnel Psychology*, Vol. 59, No. 3, Autumn 2006, pp. 623–664.

Staten, Michael E., and John M. Barron, *Evaluating the Effectiveness of Credit Counseling: Phase One: The Impact of Delivery Channels for Credit Counseling Services*, May 31, 2006. As of July 6, 2007: http://www.consumerfed.org/pdfs/Credit_Counseling_Report061206.pdf

Sullivan, Patrick, "Gender Differences and the Online Classroom: Male and Female College Students Evaluate Their Experiences," *Community College Journal of Research and Practice*, Vol. 25, No. 10, 2001, pp. 805–818.

U.S. Code, Title 11, Section 111, Nonprofit Budget and Credit Counseling Agencies; Financial Management Instructional Courses, revised April 29, 2005.

U.S. Department of Justice, U.S. Trustee Program, "Instructions for Application for Approval as a Nonprofit Budget and Credit Counseling Agency," OMB 1105-0084, July 5, 2006. As of July 6, 2007: http://www.usdoj.gov/ust/eo/bapcpa/ccde/docs/CC_Application_Instructions.pdf

U.S. Government Accountability Office, *Bankruptcy Reform: Value of Credit Counseling Requirement Is Not Clear*, GAO-07-203, April 6, 2007. As of July 6, 2007: http://www.gao.gov/new.items/d07203.pdf

U.S. Senate, Committee on Homeland Security and Governmental Affairs, Permanent Subcommittee on Investigations, *Profiteering in a Non-Profit Industry: Abusive Practices in Credit Counseling: Report*, Washington, D.C.: U.S. Government Printing Office, Senate report 109-55, April 13, 2005. As of July 6, 2007: http://purl.access.gpo.gov/GPO/LPS62165

USTP—*see* U.S. Department of Justice, U.S. Trustee Program.

Visa USA, *Credit Counseling: Debt Management Plan Analysis*, January 1999.

Weekes, Sue, "If It Moves, Measure It," *Training and Coaching Today*, April 2006, pp. 16–17.

Zhan, M., S. G. Anderson, and J. Scott, "Financial Knowledge of the Low-Income Population: Effects of a Financial Education Program," *Journal of Sociology and Social Welfare*, Vol. 33, No. 1, 2006, pp. 53–74.